THE WORLD'S STUPIDEST GRAFFITI

THE WORLD'S STUPIDEST GRAFFITI

Michael O'Mara Humour

First published in Great Britain in 2002 by
Michael O'Mara Books Limited
9 Lion Yard
Tremadoc Road
London SW4 7NQ

A CIP catalogue record for this book is available
from the British Library

ISBN 1-85479-876-6

1 3 5 7 9 10 8 6 4 2

Designed and typeset by Design 23

www.mombooks.com

Printed and bound in Great Britain by Cox & Wyman,
Reading, Berks

CONTENTS

graffito: *n*. 1 Archaeol. any inscription or drawing scratched or carved onto a surface, esp. rock or pottery.

graffiti: *pl*. drawings, messages, etc. often obscene, scribbled on the walls of public lavatories, advertising posters, etc. [C19: from the Italian: a little scratch, from *graffio*.]

POLITICS

Question
Authority –
Don't ask why,
just DO IT!

Politicians are
Those who deal
with The
problems That
Would not exist
if They
didn'T exisT

I try to see
things the
government's way

But you can't get
your head up
your butt

Earth is
~~full~~ –
go home

STOP
GLOBAL
WHINING

Bureaucracy- transforming energy into solid waste

RELIGION

JESUS LOVES
YOU

just not in that way

Jesus loves you,
but everyone else thinks
you're an asshole

Jesus is coming!
Look busy!

JESUS SAVES
SINNERS

and redeems them for
valuable cash prizes

If God is within
I hope he likes
enchiladas

God is a
single parent

Eve was ~~framed~~

God is coming
And is
SHE mad!!

There is no
room for
God in my
world
Probably why
he has a nice
place of his
own

May God bless those who love us. And those who do not love us, may He turn their hearts. And if He does not turn their hearts, may He turn their ankles so we may know them by their limping.

WORK

If you're happy
and you know it
clank your
chains..!

If you can't beat them, arrange to have them *beaten*

Where there's a whip, there's a way

The beatings will
continue until
morale improves

If you have something
to say, raise your
right hand
... and cover your
mouth with it

Two rules for success
1. Never tell all you
know

Work smarter
not harder and
watch your
speling!

Nothing's impossible if you're not the one who has to do it

Get it done by Friday!

Robinson Crusoe

Top Ten reasons to procrastinate

1.

for every action
there is an equal
and opposite
criticism

Mediocre people are always at their best

Don'T use a big word where a diminuTive one will suffice

You can fool
some of the
people some of
the time ...

...THOSE ARE THE ONES TO
CONCENTRATE ON

If at first you don't
succeed,
destroy all evidence
that you tried

If at first you do
succeed,
try not to look
astonished

Eagles may soar,
but weasels
don't get sucked
into jet engines

ANOTHER DEADLINE,
ANOTHER MIRACLE

To err
is human

To forgive is against company policy

If at first you
don't succeed,
skydiving is not
for you

Always proofread.
You might have
something out

Work is for people
who don't
SURF THE NET

Seven out of ten
voices in my head say
"Call in sick"

I used up all
my sick days,
so I'm calling
in dead.

WORK is for
people who don't
know how to
FISH

Telepath wanted: you know where to apply

I owe it all to my boss – ulcers, nausea, paranoia...

All work and no play will make you a manager

A closed mouth gathers no feet

Admit nothing, deny everything, make counter accusations

PROCRASTINATE LATER

Don't suffer from stress...

Be a carrier

Death is life's way of telling you you've been fired

I.T.

Set your
laser printer
to stun

I THINK THEREFORE IMAC

Wherever I hang my @ that's my home

I have NOT lost my mind.

It's backed up on the server

(and the network is
down again...)

Computers cut my work in half... and the boss expects me to put it all back together!

The information went data way

The Definition of an Upgrade: Take old bugs out, put new ones in

Access denied- nah nah na nah nah!

C:\> Bad
command or file
name!
Go stand in the
corner

Disinformation is not
as good as
datinformation

SENILE.COM
found . . .

Out Of
Memory . . .

ASCII stupid
question, get a
stupid ANSI!

READ MY CHIPS:
NO NEW
UPGRADES!

Hit any user to continue

I hit the CTRL key but I'm still not in control!

Will the information superhighway have any rest stops?

I dropped my computer on my foot! That Megahurtz!

RELATIONSHIPS:

To all virgins
Thanks for
nothing

If you want my respect get on your knees and beg for it

Sex is hereditary - if your parents didn't have it neither will you

The problem with
sex in the movies
is your popcorn
usually spills

PRINCESS WITH
ENOUGH EXPERIENCE
OF PRINCES -
SEEKS FROG

WITH FRIENDS LIKE THESE WHO NEEDS ENEMAS?

Be nice to your kids – they'll choose your nursing home

Kids in the back seat cause accidents

Accidents in the back seat cause kids

The sex was so good that even the neighbours had a cigarette

IF YOU SMOKE AFTER SEX, YOU'RE DOING IT TOO FAST

GROW YOUR OWN DOPE, PLANT A MAN

Guys have feelings too

but like . . . who cares?

I almost had a psychic girlfriend but she left me before we met

WANTED:
Meaningful overnight relationship

Women exist
because sheep
can't cook

Men exist
because cats
won't mow
the lawn

DON'T HATE YOURSELF IN THE MORNING — SLEEP TILL NOON!

So many men,
so little reason
to sleep with any
of them

Most men would respect a woman's mind more if it bounced gently as she walked

Nine out of ten men who have tried camels prefer women

A Real Friend isn't someone that you use once and throw away, a Real Friend is someone that you can use again and again!

FRIENDS HELP YOU MOVE. REAL FRIENDS HELP YOU MOVE BODIES

How many roads must a man walk down before he admits he is lost?

WOMEN WANT ME.
FISH FEAR ME

Marry not a
tennis player.
For love means
nothing to them

He who hesitates is not only lost, but miles from the next exit

and probably male

While I wait
for the
perfect woman
to come along,
I'm having a
lot of fun with
the imperfect
ones!

IMPOTENCE: NATURE'S WAY OF SAYING "NO HARD FEELINGS"

Nothing is better than sex. Masturbation is better than nothing. Therefore, masturbation is better than sex

STREET
WISDOM

A journey of a thousand
miles begins with a cash
advance

There's no
Police like
Holmes

Condense
soup, not
books!

I don't deserve self-esteem

Blessed be the censors, for they shall inhibit the Earth

If tomorrow never comes, then you're dead

All things are possible!

except skiing through

a revolving door

Every morning is
the dawn of a
new error

It is better to
have loafed and
lost than never to
have loafed at all

Cats are smarter than dogs. They refuse to pull a sled

Cats remind us that not everything has a purpose

Captain Kirk, meet
my father.
He's Dad, Jim

**Those who live by the
sword get shot by those
who don't**

Please do not feed
the ego

Alcohol and calculus
don't mix
NEVER DRINK
AND DERIVE

Beer – helping
white people dance
since the
Middle Ages

REHAB IS FOR QUITTERS

Life in a vacuum sucks!

Beauty is in the eye of the beerholder!

CHAOS –
More Than a
Theory, iT's
The Way of
Life

CLOSET

EXTROVERT

Just say No to negativism

JUST SAY NO THANK YOU!

(Miss Manners)

You can't have everything – where would you put it?

Time is a great healer, but a lousy beautician

Cleanliness is next
to impossible

Youth is
fleeting, but
immaturity
can last a
lifetime

What doesn't kill you
merely postpones the
inevitable

If you can smile
when Things go
wrong, you
have someone in
mind To blame

When everyThing's
coming your way —
you're going The
wrong way up a
one-way sTreeT

The early bird
gets the worm,
but the second mouse
gets the cheese

It's tough at the top!

*Sure, and it's a party
at the bottom*

Red meat is bad
for you.

No, fuzzy, green meat
is bad for you!

SMOKING CURES HAM

On the other hand... there are five different fingers

It's so
cold here,
the lawyers
have their
hands in
their own
pockets!

Every 10 seconds,
somewhere on
this Earth,
there is a woman
giving birth to a
child.
*She must be found
and stopped*

Support bacteria —
it's the only
culture some
people have

Cole's law:
thinly sliced
cabbage

Santa's elves are just a bunch of subordinate clauses

Cure insomnia - get more sleep

The best way to talk to a lion is by long-distance telephone.

Sorry, lion's busy.

SHOPLIFTERS HAVE THE GIFT OF THE GRAB

Is there intelligent life on Earth?

Yes, but I'm only visiting !

I FOUGHT THE LAWN AND THE LAWN WON

Communicate
with a fish
drop it a line

I'd give my right
hand to be
ambidextrous

WHY, OH WHY, OH WHY?

If space is a vacuum
who changes the bag?

What if there were no hypothetical questions?

Why doesn't Tarzan have a beard?

If Barbie is so popular, why do you have to buy her friends?

What was the best thing before sliced bread?

How deep would the ocean be without the sponges?

If one synchronized
swimmer drowns,
do the rest have to
drown too?

Why does
Christmas always
come when the
shops are so busy?

Is French kissing just kissing in France?

I JUST WANT REVENGE – IS THAT SO WRONG?

Is it possible to be a closet claustrophobic?

Can blue men sing the whites?

If Dracula has no reflection, how come he always has such a straight parting?

LIFE

Abandon the search
for truth,
look for a good

fantasy

CLONES
ARE PEOPLE
TWO

Plan to be

spontaneous

tomorrow

Two wrongs never make a right

BUT TWO WRIGHTS
MADE AN AEROPLANE

Denial is not a river in Egypt

Honk if you love peace and quiet

I can see clearly now, the brain is gone...

So many stupid people, so few comets

HEARTLESS
MOCKERY
PRACTISED
HERE

Forgive
and
~~forget~~!

BUT KEEP A LIST OF NAMES

I do whatever
my rice crispies tell
me to

All stressed out and
no one to choke!

Humpty Dumpty
was pushed

In space, your cat can't hear you open the can

Selective hearing: it works for me!

It's a control freak
thing. I won't let
you understand!

Proudly march
to the beat of a
different kettle
of fish

Never play
leapfrog with a
unicorn

One by one the

penguins steal

my sanity

Love your enemies,
it really gets
them confused

MADNESS TAKES
ITS TOLL.
PLEASE HAVE
EXACT CHANGE

Therapy is expensive, popping bubble wrap is cheap.
You choose

RELISH TODAY, KETCHUP TOMORROW

Time flies like
an arrow
Fruit flies like
a banana

FAT HAPPENS

NONCONFORMISTS

ARE ALL ALIKE

Those who forget
the pasta are
condemned to
reheat it

I used to be a

Kleptomaniac but I

took something for it

I'm an optimist but I don't think it helps much!

Always borrow money from a pessimist – they don't expect you to pay them back

I'M NOT A PESSIMIST. I'M OPTIMISTICALLY CHALLENGED

I know the voices aren't real, but they have some good ideas

ROCK IS DEAD

long live paper and scissors

ELEVATOR OUT OF ORDER. TRY THE ONES ACROSS THE STREET

I get enough
exercise just
pushing my luck !

Witch Parking,
all others will
be toad

Deja Moo: The feeling you've heard this bull before!

Sign at a Petrol Pump:
FRIENDLY SELF SERVICE!

Tolkien is hobbit-forming

Yorick is a numb-skull

Always avoid alliteration

Today's pigs are tomorrow's bacon

BE ALERT—
YOUR COUNTRY
NEEDS LERTS

Nothing is more wasted than a smile... on the face of a Playmate centrefold.

THE APPLIANCE OF SCIENCE:

Gravity...not just
a good idea:
It's the LAW!

There is no such thing as gravity, the Earth sucks!

A vibration is a motion that can't make up its mind which way it wants to go.

Entropy: Not just a fad, it's the future!

Time is what keeps everything from happening at once

Quantum Mechanics: the dreams stuff is made of

Photons have mass!??
I didn't even know
they were Catholic...

If you're not part of the solution, you're part of the precipitate

All that glitters has a high refractive index

Black holes are
where God
divided by zero

BARIUM: WHAT
YOU DO WITH
DEAD CHEMISTS

THE

RULES:

JAMES BOND

RULES OOK!

DYSLEXIA RULES, K.O.

DYSLEXICS UNTIE

DYSLEXICS HAVE MORE FNU

AMNESIA RULES, OOOO....

ESCALATORS ARE
ON THE WAY UP

EXITS ARE ON
THE WAY OUT

Nostalgia rules, hokey cokey

And the meek shall inherit the earth, as long as nobody minds

BATHROOM WALLS

We aim to please!
You aim too! Please!

Sign posted in a bathroom

Welcome to our ool.
Notice there's no P in it.
Please keep it that way

Sign seen at a swimming pool

ANAL INTERCOURSE
IS FOR ASSHOLES

Don't look up here,
the joke's in your hand.

Written high upon the wall above a urinal

Don't buy this gum, it tastes like rubber

Scratched into the paint of the
condom-dispensing machine

All Michael O'Mara titles are available by post from:
Bookpost, P.O. Box 29, Douglas, Isle of Man IM99 1BQ

Credit cards accepted.
Please telephone 01624 836000
Fax 01624 837033
Internet http://www.bookpost.co.uk

Free postage and packing in the UK.
Overseas customers allow £1 per book (paperbacks)
And £3.00 per book (hardbacks)

Other humour titles:
The World's Stupidest Criminals – ISBN 1-85479-879-0
The World's Stupidest Men – ISBN 1-85479-508-2
The World's Stupidest Laws – ISBN 1-85479-549-X
The World's Stupidest Signs – ISBN 1-85479-555-4
The Book of Urban Legends – ISBN 1-85479-932-0
Outrageous Expressions – ISBN 1-85479-556-2
Totally Stupid Men – ISBN 1-85479-274-1
Stupid Men Quiz Book – ISBN 1-85479-693-3
Complete Crap – ISBN 1-85479-313-6
Wicked Cockney Rhyming Slang – ISBN 1-85479-386-1
All Men Are Bastards – ISBN 1-85479-387-X
The Ultimate Book of Farting – ISBN 1-85479-596-1
The Complete Book of Farting – ISBN 1-85479-440-X
The History of Farting – ISBN 1-85479-754-9
The Ultimate Insult – ISBN 1-85479-288-1
The Little Englander's Handbook – ISBN 1-85479-553-8